Appliance Handbook For

Women

Simple Enough Even Men Can Understand

by

Vernon Schmidt

authorHOUSE™
1663 LIBERTY DRIVE, SUITE 200
BLOOMINGTON, INDIANA 47403
(800) 839-8640
WWW.AUTHORHOUSE.COM

First published by AuthorHouse 05/23/05

ISBN: 1-4208-5957-9 (e)
ISBN: 1-4208-3454-1 (sc)

Printed in the United States of America
Bloomington, Indiana

This book is printed on acid-free paper.

Contents

If you own any appliance or are planning
to purchase any appliance in the future this
book is guaranteed to save you money.

EVERYTHING YOU NEED TO KNOW ABOUT
REPLACING OR REPAIRING YOUR APPLIANCE

NOW YOU CAN KNOW WHAT THE SALES PEOPLE
DIDN'T TELL YOU -- WHAT THE MANUFACTURES
DON'T PUT IN THE OWNER'S MANUALS -- HOW
TO SAVE MONEY ON UNNEEDED SERVICE CALLS -
- AND GET THE TRUTH ABOUT YOUR APPLIANCES
FROM AN AUTHORIZED SERVICE TECHNICIAN
WITH 28 YEARS OF EXPERIENCE.

The Homeowners Handbook

If you don't have money to throw away, read this book before you call for any in-home service on your major household appliances or heating and air conditions system. Are you tired of paying ridiculous prices for service just to find out there was a simple solution to your problem? This book can save you hundreds of dollars in unnecessary repairs.

Before you call for service you can research your complaint by looking it up and finding out if there is an easy solution to your problem.

Several service calls are run each day and consumers are charged for simple things that have nothing to do with mechanical problems.

Now you can look up the type of appliance and find the easy fix for a fraction of what it cost just to have a technician show up at your door.

- DISHES DON'T COME OUT CLEAN FROM YOUR DISHWASHER?
- CLOTHES TAKE FOREVER TO GET DRY IN YOUR DRYER?
- WASHER NOT SPINNING OUT ALL THE WATER FROM YOUR CLOTHES?

- MICROWAVE MAKING FUNNY NOISES?
- YOUR RANGE ISN'T COOKING CORRECTLY?

These and many more problems can be solved by following some simple steps and without ever touching a tool.

Just look up the type of appliance find the complaint that matches your problem and read and follow the solution.

Every day people are taking time off work or out of their schedules and being charged anywhere from $30.00 to $80.00 for a service call that could be avoided just by using this simple-to-follow guide.

Chapter 1
TODAY'S NEW
APPLIANCES

Today's new appliances are more energy efficient with more options than ever before. They are made of lighter materials, more electronics and most are easier to service. All this and they are one of the few things that you can still buy for about the same price as you could 15 years ago. It is important to understand the differences between new appliances today and appliances that you have owned previously. One of the key things to keep in mind is that appliances have not gone up in cost like most everything else over the past twenty years. Does this mean they will not last as long as the old appliances? Not necessarily. If you follow the tips and advice in this book you can save a lot of money and get the most out of your new appliance. Remember that the warranty that comes with your new appliance will in most cases only cover the service call if there is actually a problem with the appliance.

Women are always talking about how men will not stop to ask for directions even when they are lost, which in most cases may be true. We men believe we know what we are doing and can figure it out. I have found that women have that same instinct when it comes to their appliances and in some cases, just like men, will sometimes find their destination. Women can work an appliance without directions. But keep in mind if the appliance is not doing what you believe it should, you need to read the Owner's Manual before you call for service. Your warranty will not cover a service call for customer instruction.

This means if you call for service on your new appliance and the problem or noise you called about is covered in the owner's manual as a normal condition for that appliance, **you** have to pay for the service call. **Always** be sure to read your owner's manual trouble shooting guide before you call for service. For over twenty-six years I have serviced both new and used appliances. The problems have changed but the amount of service on new appliances is about the same. Just because you never had to have service on your old appliance when it was new, doesn't mean that your new appliance is not just as good. For twenty-six years I've stayed very busy repairing new appliances, so obviously everyone wasn't as lucky as you were in the past. There have been many changes in today's appliances. Most appliances are becoming more electronic with more options and therefore have more things that could possibly breakdown. At the beginning of each chapter I will explain some of the major differences about that particular appliance, what you should expect from that particular appliance and what you can do to prolong the life of your new and more energy efficient appliance.

Today's new appliances use less electricity, less water and have several options that were not available on the older appliances. Most of this has been achieved without raising the cost of appliances. There are much more expensive appliances available. But, if you compare today's models with similar models ten to fifteen years ago you'll find the prices have not changed much. In some cases, the prices are lower today than they were in the past. The main difference you'll find in today's appliances is that they make different noises and sometimes more noise than your old appliance did. This is because today's appliances have more plastic and thinner metal than the older appliances.

Replacing your old appliances is still a major purchase and should be handled accordingly; you should do some research before making your decision. Most customers feel the sales people they are dealing with should tell them everything they need to know about the new product they are buying. The fact is that even the best trained and most honest sales people only have limited knowledge about every item they sell. Even the most experienced service tech can not tell you everything about all the different makes and models out there. One thing I have found is that some of the machines that seem to have the least amount of service in one area are the ones that have the most in other areas. And just because someone tells you one brand or model seems to have the most service does not always mean it is any worse than other models. It may just be that more of them are being sold. It has always been the brand that sells the most gets the most service.

I subscribe to *Consumer Reports* just to keep up on what they are saying but you should not limit your research to just *Consumer Reports*. They are not always right. Ask friends about their appliances and talk to different sales people at different locations and, if possible, talk to <u>service</u> people about models you are interested in. Listen to the good and bad from the sales people then compile all this information to help you find the model that is right for you.

Several problems that may occur with your new appliance may have nothing to do with the actual appliance but how and where this appliance is installed. Remember that because this appliance is built with less metal it is going to be lighter weight and therefore react differently in the same place that your old appliance was installed. If your appliance is being installed in a new home keep in mind that today's houses are built differently than older homes. This means that even your old appliance may not work the same in a new home as it did in your old home. You will find better examples of this listed in the following chapters. Overall you will find that your new appliance will still last several years if you follow the simple guidelines listed in each category of the following chapters.

Service vs. Replacement

At some point you are going to come to this cross road. I have seen many customers that believe it is a waste of money to have a service tech come out to do a repair. Sometimes that is true. Look over the physical condition of your appliance before you call for service. If you see rust, broken or missing parts such as shelves, handles, knobs and so forth then it may be time to look at replacing the appliance. But if your appliances are under 10 years old and in good shape the repair might be much less than the cost of replacement. Of course you will need to make sure you have an honest repair person to do the job. See chapter 12 for tips on this.

There are a lot of service techs that will tell you that you are better off to spend the money to keep your old machine going because it is better made than a new one. You have to decide that based on the physical condition and how well you like the appliance. This is what I tell my customers when they ask for my opinion. If your appliance is 10 years old or older and the total repair is more than a third of the price of a new one, then you may be wasting money to repair it. If one part is bad on a machine that age, all the other parts also have the same wear and may or may not be far behind on needing to be replaced. If you really like the appliance and want to fix it keep in mind that only the bad part is being replaced. If any other part fails down the road it will cost additional to replace it. You may end up spending more to repair it over the long run than to replace it now.

I have also run into customers that will call for service and pay the price for a service call and not be willing to spend any money to have the repair done. Keep in mind that to have any appliance checked out you will have to pay at least a service charge or trip charge. No reputable company will send a tech to your house and spend the time to properly check your appliance for free. If you are not going to fix the appliance for any price don't waste your money for a service call. Also keep in mind when looking into replacement that there are other costs to include for things like delivery and installation. Be sure to include all of these costs into your decision.

Chapter 2
DISHWASHERS

1. New Dishwashers

2. Film on the dishes after cycle

3. Glasses and silverware are spotty

4. Water leaks sometimes

5. Funny noise when running

6. Dishes not drying

1. New dishwashers

The favorite appliance in the kitchen. Today's new dishwashers use less water and less electricity than older models. They have a lot more options but require a little more care than some of the older models. If you read this section carefully and follow the tips provided, your new dishwasher will do a good job and save you time and money.

When shopping for a new dishwasher keep in mind the most expensive models that have all bells and whistles still will require following these tips to get good clean dishes and make your new dishwasher last. The lower price models will clean your dishes, they are noisier and do not have as many spray jets or options but they still beat washing by hand. More expensive models are quieter and have more options such as heated dry and temperature boost, a big plus in getting clean dishes. Hot water supply is one of the most important things for your dishwasher. The older models would heat up to 150 degrees or more on the temperature boost, but don't expect that in your new one. Do not get caught up in the latest commercials on soap products and dishwashers. Remember . . . it is a commercial. Have you seen the burgers on fast food commercials? Now, have you ever seen one that looked like that in the restaurant? I rest my case.

I have found most people would rather have their refrigerator or range out of service than their dishwasher. We have become a very spoiled society, myself included. Your dishwasher is probably one of the most convenient appliances you own. It doesn't matter if it is the most expensive or the cheapest model available, it will last several years with the proper care. Keep in mind the cheaper models will be noisier and they will not have as many options but they will clean your dishes if you follow some simple advice.

First, always scrape your dishes to remove large food particles from them. You don't have to pre-clean the dishes, but don't put garbage in the dishwasher. Maybe you were told your dishwasher has a built in garbage disposal. Well, it is not designed to remove large portions of food. If you put food in your dishwasher you will soon have little tiny food particles drying on your dishes at the end of the cycle.

Next, and most important, do not use too much soap. I know most owner's manuals will say to fill up your soap cups. In twenty-six years I have never seen a dishwasher that requires that much soap. Today's detergents are much more concentrated and will cause several problems if you use too much. Soaps do not dissolve well unless you start each cycle with water temperatures of 130 degrees in your dishwasher. Scrape the food off your dishes before loading in the dishwasher. Start with just one half teaspoon of soap in each soap cup. If your dishes are not clean you can increase the amount but you should never need more than one tablespoon in each soap cup. For more on this see the section on "Dishes have film on them at the end of the cycle." If you follow these suggestions you will find your dishwasher will do a better job for a much longer time.

To make this simple I will list the most common complaints that are received from consumers on their dishwashers and after the complaint I will list the most probable cause of the problems and what you can do to remedy the problems.

2. My dishes have a film left on them at the end of the cycle.

You are using too much soap; more soap does not mean cleaner dishes in your dishwasher. There is an easy test to find out if you're using too much soap. First, open your dishwasher after it has set overnight and wipe your hand over the inside panel of the door. If you have a white powdery film on your hand you are using too much soap. Next, look closely at the spray arms inside your dishwasher. Check to see if the small holes in the spray arm are stopped up with soap. If the holes are plugged you are using too much soap. If these check okay, do the final test. Run the hot water at your kitchen sink until the water coming out of the faucet is good and hot. Now start your dishwasher at the beginning of the cycle and let it run for three to four minutes then stop it by opening the door. Look close at the water in the bottom of the dishwasher for any soap bubbles or soapy film on top of the water. If you find any soapy residue in the water you are using too much soap. Ninety percent of the customers I service use more soap than needed in their dishwasher. If you have soft water, you only need to use about one teaspoon of detergent for the full load of dishes. If you have hard water you'll need to use about one tablespoon of detergent. You will notice I said one teaspoon of detergent. To help you better understand why you do not need very much detergent to clean your dishes, let's discuss your dishwasher.

I know, you say your old dishwasher worked fine with filling the soap cups up. Well, your old dishwasher used a lot more water with every fill. The newer your dishwasher the less water it uses. Today's soaps are a lot more concentrated and they are scientifically designed to remove food particles from your dishes. Most people rinse most of the food off the dishes before loading them in the dishwasher. The dishwasher cleans the dishes by spraying pressurized hot water over the dishes. You only need detergent to loosen any dried food particles left on the dishes. The hot water spraying over the dishes does the rest. Try using less soap. You have nothing to loose and you will save money. Read on to find out how to get the extra soap out of the dishwasher.

I have customers argue that soap can not be the problem. They say that they have tried less soap. If you have used too much soap you must get the soap build up out before you add any soap. To remove soap build up in your dishwasher you will need to run a dishwasher cleaner through the unit. Dishwasher cleaners a fairly new to the market; they can be found at most grocery stores in the dishwasher detergent area. *Jett Dry* and *Glisten* both make a dishwasher cleaner. Do not confuse *Jett Dry Rise Aid* with the cleaner. Both brands should be available at your supermarket along with the dishwashing detergents. You will need to run at least one box of cleaner through to remove the soap build up from inside your dishwasher. Additional boxes may be needed if you have heavy build up. I advise my customers to run this cleaner through at least one time every thirty days if they have hard water and at least one time every ninety days if they have soft water. This will help to keep the inside of the dishwasher clean and also keeps the inside of the pump and spray arms free and open. The most common cause of early dishwasher failure is from constantly using too much soap.

3. Glasses and silverware are very spotted.

Hard water or no rinse aid. If you have hard water you may not be able to get rid of water spots. Try using the following tips. You should consider adding a water softener to your home. A water softener will make all your water-using appliances and all your water pipes and faucets last longer.

There are some things you can do to help eliminate spots even with hard water. Make sure your liquid rinse aid dispenser is full. Keep in mind that only a few drops of rinse aid is dispensed in the rinse cycle so you should only have to add more to the dispenser about once a month. You will need to call for service if your rinse aid is not dispensing. If your dispenser is working and you still have spots try using *Glass Magic*, a water-conditioning additive with your detergent. Be sure not to add too much. Use equal parts of detergent and *Glass Magic*. For example, use one teaspoon of detergent and one teaspoon of *Glass Magic*.

You may not be able to find *Glass Magic* in some parts of the country due to environmental issues, but if it is available you should be able to find it with the dishwashing detergents. If you have soft water you should only need to use the liquid rinse aid in the dispenser built in your dishwasher. If you are using the liquid rinse aid dispenser and you still have spots you may be using too much soap.

4. Sometimes there is water leaking from the dishwasher, leaving a puddle on the floor.

Dishes are stacked wrong on bottom rack or jets on the spray arms are stopped up.

Using to much soap or the wrong soap.

It is best to stack only plates or small thin items in the front part of the lower rack. Be sure to stack them vertically from front to back. Stacking them from side to side will cause water to ricochet off them and leak from under the door. This will cause a small puddle in front of your dishwasher at the end of the cycle.

Also check to make sure that the holes in the spray arms are not stopped up or restricted by any particles that may have been floating in your dishwasher water. This will also cause water to leak out from under the door.

Your dishwasher will also leak if you have soap built up in the system (see film on dishes)

Be sure that no dishes that have been in the sink with hand soap or regular dish soap on them have worked their way inside the dishwasher. This will cause soapsuds to overflow and leak out the door. If dishes have been sitting in the sink, rinse them off to make sure there is no soap residue on them before loading in the dishwasher.

5. Dishwasher makes a funny noise when running.

Broken pieces of dishes have worked their way into the food disposer blade area.

Some dishwashers have a sump area that can be cleaned to remove these items; others have to have the top portion of the pump removed. In either case it may be best to have a qualified service technician to do this because you may cause more damage to your pump if it is not done properly. Sometimes the noise is coming from the motor, which in most case means the motor/pump assembly will need to be changed.

6. Dishes are wet after the dry cycle.

Today's dishwashers do not get as hot as the older models; thus they use less energy to operate.

Make sure all cups and glassware are tilted to insure water does not pool in the dips on the bottom of them. Be sure you have the heated dry option turned on. Some models require that this option be selected at the beginning of the cycle each time you turn on the dishwasher. Most new dishwashers will not get hot enough to dry any plastics in your unit. If you have one of the more expensive models it may have a vent that opens during the dry cycle and then closes at the end of the cycle. You can check your owner's manual to find out if your model comes with this feature. If it does you will need to unload the dishwasher as close as possible to the end of the dry cycle. If you leave the dishes in too long after the cycle ends, moisture from down inside the pump will build back up on your dishes.

Remember these are only the most common complaints and problems you can fix without having to pay a service technician to come to your home and charge you a hefty service fee. There are many other things that can go wrong with your dishwasher that will require a qualified service technician to repair. See the section on "Finding a qualified service company" for more help with this.

Chapter 3
DRYERS

1. New dryers

2. Taking too long to dry

3. No heat

4. Makes too much noise

5. Inside of drum discolored

6. Dryer cabinet gets hot to the touch

7. Runs too long after clothes are dry

8. Will not start - dead

1. New dryers

New dryers use a lot less energy to run than older dryers. The newer the dryer the more this is true. Because of that, the newer dryers require some different hook ups than your older dryer. Venting is the most important thing on your dryer, old or new. The vent going out of your house needs to be 4" in diameter and has to be keep clean all the way through to keep you dryer running properly. Many people believe that the lint filter catches all the lint. This has never been true. The older dryers never caught all the lint. The biggest difference is today's newer washers don't filter lint. They agitate the clothes a lot faster loosening a lot more lint from the clothing. Thus, your dryer has to remove all the lint. Newer clothing, like everything else, is different and most fabrics release more lint. So now your dryer is sucking out a lot more lint and filling your vent with more lint. You can read more about cleaning your vent in section 2 of this chapter.

You may also hear some strange noises in your new dryer. Some of these are normal due to the changes made in manufacturing. To find out if the noise is a normal noise for that dryer, refer to the owner's manual. If the noise is not described in the owner's manual, call the manufacturer at the number listed in the owner's manual. Many people call where they purchased the product and ask the sales person or the service counter people. It is rare that these people would know if your model is supposed to make a certain noise. Your best bet is to call the manufacturer to be sure. Remember your warranty will not cover a service call on your new product if the product is not actually broken. Your newer dryer does not get as hot as the older ones and they use more air and less heat to do the job. The newer washers spin the clothes out a lot faster so they are not as wet going into the dryer. If you purchase a new dryer and keep a older washer you may find it takes a little longer to dry due to the fact your older washer does not spin as fast as the newer ones. Don't confuse this with having a restricted vent. See section 2 on "takes too long to dry" to be sure. If your dryer is hooked up properly and you keep your vent cleaned you will get several years of use and most likely will never have a service call.

2. Taking too long to dry

If your dryer is taking too long to dry, the number 1 cause is a restricted vent. Your dryer requires a certain amount of airflow to work properly.

There are other things that can cause the dryer to take to long to dry but they are not as common. We will go over them to help if the dryer vent checks ok.

First, let's check your vent. The easiest way to determine if your vent is the problem is to pull the dryer out from the wall and disconnect the vent hose. Now keep the dryer out least a couple of feet from the wall and put a load in it and run it to see if the load dries in a normal amount of time. If it does your problem is in the vent somewhere; we will go over how to clean your vent in a minute. If the load still takes too long you may have a bad thermostat or timer or possibly a bad seal. Some dryers have dual heaters and one of the heaters could be bad. Most of these problems will require taking the dryer apart to find the bad part so you may need to call for service. Just be sure when you are testing the dry time with the vent disconnected that the dryer is not too close to the wall and you do not have the airflow restricted.

You will have some lint come out from the back of the dryer but not a lot. It will be cheaper to clean up a little lint than to pay a service call just to be told that the dryer is fine and you have a restricted vent.

If you don't want to clean up lint you can go to about any hardware store and purchase an indoor vent kit. It has a short hose and a small bucket with vent holes. You connect the hose to the back of the dryer, then to the bucket, put a small amount of water in the bucket and run your dryer. The water will catch the lint and the air will escape out the vent holes into the room. This will let you test your dryer for the cost of the indoor vent kit, under $10.00 almost anywhere, with out getting lint flying around your room.

Now let's talk about how to clean your vent. The quickest way is to use a leaf or yard blower. This may not work if you have a lot of buildup but it's worth a try. With your dryer pulled out from the wall, remove the hose from the dryer but leave it attached to the wall. Now put the tube of the blower inside the hose that you have taken off the dryer. Next put some type of tape such as duct tape around the hose to secure it to the tube and force all the air to go to the outside.

Now you will need to find out where your vent comes out of your house.

If you turn on the blower it might help, you will see the flaps moving from the air, you may need a ladder to get to the vent and some vents actually go up through the roof. You will need to get to the end of the vent, and with the blower on, forcing the air out, you will need to pick the lint out from around the flaps or screens.

If there are no big gobs of lint coming out and you feel a lot of air, you have lint sticking to the pipe and the blower will not take that off. Remember you tested the dryer and we have determined that without the vent hooked up it works fine so now we need to concentrate on getting the vent properly cleaned.

From here you will have to either take the vent apart and clean it or replace it. If you can get to the vent, it is not hard to clean or replace. But, if you are not sure, you may need to call handy man or service company.

3. No heat

A dryer that is not heating at all may have a simple fix. First you need to know if your dryer is a gas or electric model. If it is electric, you need to make sure you have the proper voltage going to it. First thing to check is the breaker switch box or fuse box. Your dryer can still run and not heat if the right amount of voltage is not at the dryer. If you have breakers, find the one for the dryer and turn it off and then back on, this will reset the breaker. If you still have no heat and the dryer is running you may have a bad thermostat or heater. In this case you will have to take the dryer apart or call for service.

If you have a gas dryer be sure that the gas is turned on to the dryer. I have charged many customers for a service call over the years when the only problem was (somehow) the gas got shut off behind the dryer or a breaker switch just needed to be reset. If you are sure the gas is on then you could have a bad thermostat or gas valve. In this case you will have to take the dryer apart or call for service.

4. Makes too much noise

The first thing to remember is that the newer the dryer the more noise you may hear. This is mostly due to the thickness of metal that is used in newer machines. That along with the increased airflow of newer dryers makes the noise factor louder than older machines.

If you are hearing more noise or a different noise than you have heard before such as scraping or squeaking or rubbing, then you may have a problem.

About the only things you can do without taking the dryer apart are to check to make sure the dryer is level and be sure the vent going out of your house is not restricted.

If you have a level sit it on top of the dryer from front to back and side to side if you need to adjust the legs to level the machine they will screw in or out to the required position. When finished be sure all four legs are sitting solid on the floor. If the dryer is level and the noise is still there go to the back, remove the vent pipe and pull the dryer out a least 2 feet from the wall. Now run the dryer. If the noise is still there you will have to take the dryer apart or call for service. If the noise is not there with the vent pipe disconnected, go to section 2 on too long to dry and find out how to clean your vent properly.

The most common parts to go bad that would make noises are drum rollers, bearings, glides, pulleys, belts, seals, blowers or fan blades, and, occasionally, a motor. These parts all require taking your machine apart or a call for service to have replaced.

5. Inside of drum discoloring

The most common thing that causes this is using too much soap in your washer. More soap does not mean cleaner clothes. There are a couple of things that cause this. First remember that the older dryers did not have the clean white drums that the newer machines have. So this may not have been a problem with your old dryer even though you were doing everything the same.

If you use liquid fabric softener your drum will usually turn the same color as the fabric softener. If you use colored softener sheets the same thing occurs. Once the drum discolors it will not be white again. This will not hurt anything and the color will not get onto other clothes. It stains the drum and stays there.

If you are using too much soap you will still have soap left in your clothes at the end of the wash cycle. If this happens, the dye in the fabric of your clothes comes out when the soap filled wet clothes warm up from the heat of the dryer.

For twenty-eight years most of my customers and others have used more soap than necessary

To find out if you are using too much soap go to chapter 7 on washers.

6. Dryer cabinet gets hot to the touch

Two things can cause this; first and most common is a restricted vent. See section 2 on "takes too long to dry." That will give you the information on how to check your vent and clean it if necessary.

Second your heater might be grounded out; this applies only to electric models. To check to see if your heater is grounded turn the timer dial to the position you would normally set to dry clothes, but do not start the dryer. Open the door and find the door switch, it will be a small button or lever around the door opening. Now with the timer set in a heating position push the door switch. If you start to see or feel the heaters come on without the dryer running the heater is grounded. It will need to be replaced.

To replace the heater you will have to take the dryer apart or call for service.

7. Runs too long after clothes are dry

This is another problem that may mean you have a restricted vent. Look in section 2 "takes too long to dry" for information on how to check and clean your vent.

Most dryers have automatic cycles, some are called sensor dry, designed to dry the clothes and shut the dryer off after the clothes are dry. This is done with thermostats and some models have moisture sensors. As the clothes get dryer the heat comes on less and the timer moves to shut the dryer off.

If you have a good clean vent and the dryer keeps on running you could have a bad timer, thermostat, sensor, sensor board, or heater. You will have to take the dryer apart to service these or call for a service company.

8. Dryer will not start, dead

This could be a voltage problem. If you have an electric model you need to check your breaker or fuses. If they are ok, check the voltage at the back of the dryer where the plug comes in. You need 240 volts across the red and black terminals. If you do not have the correct voltage you may have trouble somewhere else and the dryer may be ok. For this you will need a voltage meter. If you are not sure how to test voltage, call for service.

One of the most common problems that will cause the dryer not to start is a bad or broken door switch. Open the door and look for the switch button or lever. Inspect it to make sure it moves in and out freely. If it is broke it will have to be replaced.

Another thing that causes the dryer not to start is a bad thermostat or thermo fuse. To test or replace these the dryer will have to be taken apart or you will need to call for service.

Chapter 4
MICROWAVES

Today's microwaves are safer and have more options than ever before. Because of the high voltage that microwaves produce to cook with I will not include any do-it-yourself troubleshooting. I will however give you some simple test and tips to make your microwave last longer.

First and most important is to keep the inside of your microwave clean, this means under the turntable, the top and the sidewalls.

Every time you cook with your microwave it continues to cook and heat every little particle that is inside of it. If you have particles splattered on the walls from heating up last nights meatloaf, then you decide to pop some popcorn, the splatters of meatloaf will continue to cook while the popcorn is popping. Over a period of time those little splatters will finally burn the paint on the inside causing sparks inside the unit. This will cause further damage to the unit if you continue to use it.

To repair burned or shorted spots inside the unit, first clean the entire inside good with a soap and water solution, then dry the inside. If the spot is rough, use fine sandpaper to smooth it. Wipe it off well and use white appliance touch up paint to cover spot. You may have to apply a couple of coats to cover properly and then let dry for a couple of hours. Now you can begin to use your microwave again. If sparks reappear and there are no more burned spots or places that have paint scratched off then you have a more serious problem and need to call a qualified service tech.

If your microwave has a rack in it you need to remove this unless you are using it to cook with. I have seen a lot of damage to the inside caused by the rack being left inside while cooking something on the turntable. It is okay to use the rack for cooking just don't leave it in when you are not using it. Be sure that when using the rack and turntable, whatever is on the turntable does not touch it.

If you have no power to the unit it may be just a fuse inside that is bad. This will require removing the cabinet or panels to gain access inside. Since a microwave still can retain voltage after it has been unplugged it is recommended to call a qualified service tech to do even this simple repair. Remember your microwave puts out up to 4,000 volts when it is cooking, so don't experiment with trying to fix it if you are not qualified.

The simple test to see if your microwave is operating properly is to take 6 oz of water in a microwave safe cup, put it in the microwave, and set the unit to cook at full power for 2 1/2 minutes. If the water comes to a boil within this time everything is usually ok.

Chapter 5
RANGES

1. New ranges

2. Baking

3. Cleaning

4. Oven door won't unlock

1. New ranges

The big difference in the newer ranges is in the electronics. Temperatures are a lot more accurate than the older ranges so your oven will bake a little different. Your newer oven also uses more airflow than your older oven so rack adjusting is important. You may have to adjust your racks different in the new oven to get it to bake properly. You will also find that the thin cheap baking pans or sheets will not cook as even as the better ones. I have learned from experience that the thicker baking pans and sheets work better in the newer ovens. The pans that have the air channels between the inner and outer layers also due a great job. But do not throw those old cheap pans away; they are good to use to catch spillovers when baking pies and such.

The top burners are also different. You will notice that they are different sizes on both electric and gas models. If you try to use too large of a pan on a small burner or too small of a pan on a large burner it will not cook right.

On gas models you will see different size burners, besides not having the same flame these burners create more or less heat or BTU's. A small burner will not properly heat a large pan. Only the middle of the pan will get hot.

Putting a small pan on a large burner will cause the flame to go up around the edges of the pan so food in the middle will not cook properly.

If you have an electric model with the glass top your pans must be flat on the glass to cook properly. Pans that have ridges or gaps on the bottom or are warped will not cook properly on glass. To check to see if the pan is warped set it on a flat surface. Hold the rim on each side and see if it will rock. If it rocks, it is warped. You can also turn the pan upside down and use a ruler or straight edge to see it the pan is flat.

When baking remember that your newer oven will have a much more accurate temperature than the older one.

Example: a older oven set at 350 degrees would heat above the set temperature and then cool to several degrees below the set temperature to keep the baking temperature as close to 350 as possible. The newer ovens do not have that wide range of temperature fluctuations so you will keep a more constant temperature when baking. So, your older recipes may not cook the same without adjusting the time and the racks and in some cases the temperature.

2. Baking

Most people believe that if the food doesn't bake right it has something to do with the temperature. This is not always the case. The easiest way to test your oven temperature is to get an oven thermometer put in the oven leave it for 20 minutes and check it.

The owner's manual will tell you not to use this type of thermometer because they are not accurate enough. But this simple test is close enough to let you know if there is a big difference in the temperature you set and the one you are getting. Remember you will have to leave it in for at least 20 minutes to get the proper temperature reading, even though your oven will tell you it has preheated or is at temperature way before then. This doesn't mean it is taking that long to heat. It just takes that long for the thermometer to get a proper reading. If your temperature is close to what you have it set at then you probably don't need to make any adjustments.

If your temperature is more than 10 degrees off check your owner's manual on how to set or calibrate your oven temperature. On most electronic oven controls this is done by pushing certain keypads. With manual thermostats it is done with set screws on the back of the knob. Your owner's manual will walk you through the steps. Keep in mind that the manufactures warranty will not cover adjusting your thermostat even if it is off from day one.

If your temperature is correct or real close and you are still getting poor baking results you may need to make rack adjustments or buy better baking pans.

3. Cleaning

Most new ranges do not have lift up tops to clean under, an improvement most people enjoy. Gas models have sealed burners meaning they cannot be removed for cleaning. Most gas ranges have porcelain cook tops, so you can clean them without scratching the paint as long as you don't use anything too abrasive. Check your owner's manual before cleaning to be sure the top is porcelain.

To clean spillovers that won't come clean with normal hot soap and water cleaning, try spraying a little oven cleaner on a soft scrub pad and scrubbing gently. Do not spray oven cleaner directly on the top or burners and leave it. Most burners are aluminum and oven cleaner will discolor and ruin them. Check the owner's manual for more cleaning tips and warnings.

Glass top electric models require a cleaner made for them found in most stores. If you have a problem with a spot that won't come off try putting some cleaner on the spot, smooth it out but don't wipe it clean. Now take a single edge razor blade and scrape from one side. This will take off most spots that come from the bottom of your pans during cooking. For electric models with the removable coil burners clean the same as gas models.

Oven cleaning

Almost all ovens are self cleaning today. Good luck if yours is not self cleaning. Not much has been done to improve the old elbow grease method of oven cleaning.

For those of you with self-cleaning ovens pay attention. Do not use aluminum foil to line the oven bottom or racks. This will cause damage to the finish and it will not clean properly. Anytime you are baking something that might spill over it is a good ideal to put a cookie sheet under it to keep the spill over from staining the oven bottom. This will give those cheap cookie sheets that won't bake right a new use. If you do get spillovers it will not hurt the oven but it might leave a stain that won't come out.

Be sure to read your owners manual before cleaning. Remember large spillovers need to be wiped up before cleaning. Keep in mind that if you leave large spillovers in the oven they will usually catch fire during the self-clean. You cannot unlock the door to put the fire out; the door will not unlock until the oven cools down. If you do have a fire inside the oven it will burn itself out but you may have a lot of smoke damage to your house. To insure that you don't start a fire inside the oven during the self-clean cycle, wipe up all large spillovers and grease buildup before you set the self-clean cycle. Keep in mind that once your oven gets hot in the self-clean cycle you will not be able to unlock the door until the oven cools down.

Set your oven in the cleaning mode per the owner's manual. If you don't have an owner's manual it would be advisable to call the manufacturer or a parts store to purchase one. Most of the newer ovens will have automatic locks on the oven doors that will lock when you turn the oven into self-clean. If your oven has a manual lock for the oven door you will have to make sure that it is in the lock position before you can set the self-clean.

Keep in mind your oven reaches very high temperatures during self-clean. It will smell and possibly smoke, which is normal. It is best to be able to open a couple of nearby windows to air out the area.

I recommend cleaning your oven at least a couple of times a year, more if needed. Be sure to clean it a few times while it still under warranty. Because of the high temperatures during the cleaning you are more apt to have a problem during or right after the cleaning.

4. Oven door won't unlock

If your oven is self-cleaning it has a lock for the oven door. This lock should be used for self-cleaning only. Many people ruin their dinners locking the door while baking. Remember that once the oven gets hot there is a safety feature that will **not** let the door lock release until the oven cools down. If you try to force the lock open you **will** break the lock assembly. If the door will not open after the oven is cool you need to call a qualified service tech. You will do more damage and have a more costly repair trying to get the locked door open if you don't know what you are doing. Be sure to tell the service company what the make and model of the range is and be sure that they have some one with experience on locked doors.

Chapter 6
REFRIGERATORS

1. New refrigerators

2. Noisy refrigerators

3. Ice makers

4. Refrigerator not cold

5. Leaking water

1. New refrigerators

Today's new refrigerators run on a fraction of the electricity than earlier models. They have more options and in most cases are less expensive than they were fifteen years ago. That alone is quite an accomplishment.

Now let's talk about the other differences in your new refrigerator. The most common complaint is the noise and it runs too much. It probably does run more often but remember it uses a lot less power to run. It may be that you just hear it run more because it runs a little noisier than the old one. The newer high efficiency compressors make a different sound that the older models.

Like all things made today, your refrigerator is built with thinner metal and more plastic with faster moving parts and better insulation. Because of all of this combined you will hear more or at least different noises. This does not mean you have a problem. If your refrigerator is cooling fine and you hear strange noises, look in the owner's manual. Yes that's right, noise has become such a big service request that now there is a section in the owner's manual that talks about normal noises your refrigerator will make. Remember just because it doesn't sound normal to you doesn't mean that is not normal for this new refrigerator. See section 2 for "noisy refrigerators."

On the bright side, with the new insulation being used and the new ozone safe refrigerant, your new refrigerator will hold better temperatures than the older ones.

2. Noisy refrigerators

This is the most common complaint on newer refrigerators. It has a lot to do with the difference in how the newer refrigerators are constructed compared to the older ones. Your new refrigerator has a one-piece liner with no seams to leak out the cold air. Your new refrigerator has foamed in insulation, which keeps the cold in better than the fiberglass insulation in the older refrigerators, but doesn't dampen the sound as well. The metal cabinet is a lot thinner gauge metal than the older ones allowing the noise to be heard.

The cooling coils get much colder thanks to the new refrigerant, which makes them pop and crack during the defrost cycles. With all this in mind your new refrigerator is still far superior to the older ones. It will last just as long and run on a lot less electricity than the one you replaced.

In your owner's manual you will find a section on normal operating noises for your new refrigerator. Read these and you will find some explanation on what causes these noises. Remember these are normal for this new refrigerator not your old one. If the noise is not constant and comes and goes, it is probably normal. If the noise you are hearing is not listed then you may need to call for service.

If the refrigerator is cooling fine the noise may just be vibration. Be sure that the refrigerator is sitting solid on the floor; try pushing on the upper corners gently to see if the noise lessens. If it does you might try adjusting the front rollers or legs.

Remember most warranties will not cover a service call for normal operating noises. Reading the owner's manual could save you a charge for a service call.

3. Ice makers

For as long as there have been ice makers in refrigerators they have been the number one thing to have to be replaced. This is usually due to the water going to the icemaker not because the icemaker is designed to quit working every couple of years. If you are having constant icemaker problems you probably have hard water, which means you are probably having problems with other appliances. Hard water causes icemakers to go out faster. Some new refrigerators are coming out with built in water filters. But, these filters do not remove the mineral in the water, which is what causes the water to be hard. If you have a water softener then you have removed the mineral which is good, but you have added sodium which can still cause some problems with your icemaker.

The best solution is to have a water softener to soften the water and a filter, either built-in or added, on to the line coming to the refrigerator, to remove some of the sodium. This will help your icemaker last several years longer.

You can buy these add on filters at most home improvement stores for under $10, the built-in ones start at $25 and go as high as $60. Either type will do the job if you have soft water. They will have to be replaced every 6 to 12 months which is still a lot cheaper than a new icemaker.

Before we go any further you need to be sure that the water line going to your refrigerator is either copper or high pressure braided rubber or stainless. If you have the 1/4 inch white plastic water line that is so often used because it is so much easier to install, you need to replace it. I have seen thousands of dollars of damage over the years caused by this type of water line.

It will spring tiny little leaks that you will not see until major damage has already been done.

Another big problem with icemakers again which has nothing to due with the icemaker, is low water pressure coming to the refrigerator. If the water pressure is to low the icemaker will not fill properly causing hollow ice cubes that will stick and jam up the icemaker. If you notice small or hollow cubes in your ice container and then you have no ice, check your water pressure to the refrigerator.

To do this find the shut off for the water line going to the refrigerator, turn it off and disconnect the water line from the back of the refrigerator. Now get a bucket, turn the water line into the bucket and turn the water valve all the way back on. If there is plenty of pressure shooting out of the line you should be fine. If there is not much or very little pressure then that is the problem.

Usually the problem is at the valve. To be sure, disconnect the line at the valve and place your bucket to catch the water. Turn the valve on to see if you have more pressure there or is it about the same as the pressure was when the line was still hooked up. Most of the time you can replace the valve and that will take care of the problem. If you still aren't making ice after the pressure is ok then there are other things that you need to check.

Keep in mind that after you get every thing fixed it will take up to 8 hours before you will have any ice drop.

If the icemaker will not make ice you may just have a frozen fill tube. Stick your finger in the icemaker where the ice is formed. If there is no water or ice in the chamber then check the tube that fills the icemaker. You will find this tube at the back of the icemaker. With a flashlight look into the tube, if it is frozen full of ice you need to thaw it out and then wait 8 hours to see if it makes ice.

The easiest way to thaw the fill tube is to shut the refrigerator off or unplug it, then take a hair dryer and apply heat to the area where the tube is located. Continue to heat until all the ice in the tube is melted. Be sure all of the ice is melted then give it about 8 to 10 hours to make ice. If the fill tube continues to freeze up often then you need to replace the water valve on the refrigerator that goes to the ice maker. If the icemaker has ice in the chamber but will not cycle to drop the ice you probably have a bad icemaker. Be sure the temperature in the freezer is at least 10 degrees or colder. The icemaker will only cycle if the freezer is cold enough.

4. Refrigerator not cold

First thing to check is the freezer. The refrigerator gets its cold air from the freezer. If the refrigerator is not cold then most of the time the freezer is not cold enough.

If you have a thermometer, check the temperature in the freezer section. The temperature needs to be at least +10 degrees to -10 degrees in the freezer to get the refrigerator section cold enough. If you don't have a thermometer, check the ice cream, frozen juices or bread. If they are soft then the temperature in the freezer is usually not cold enough.

Look for a frost build up on the back wall of the freezer or, on some models with the freezer on top, look for the frost build up on the freezer floor. This will usually be a snowy frost. If you have the frost build up then you usually have a defrost problem. This is one of the most common problems for a not cooling refrigerator. The freezer will be cold but not keeping things frozen solid. This frost build up causes the air flow to the refrigerator to become blocked, thus causing the refrigerator to get warm since no cold air is coming from the freezer.

There are three parts to the defrost system: a timer, a heater, and a thermostat. If any of these parts go bad, you will get the same symptom. To find out which part is bad you will have to take the unit apart or call for a service company. If you have determined that this is the problem and you can't get service fast enough, there is a temporary fix you can do that will give you up to a week, maybe two, before the problem starts again. Remember that this is only a temporary fix, the problem will come back if you don't get if fixed properly.

Turn the unit off or unplug it and take every thing out of the freezer. The best way to defrost is to unplug the unit and leave the door open for 12-24 hours. If you can't store your food and it is already ruined, try the hair dryer. Using a hair dryer, thaw out all the ice in the freezer section. Remember that behind the wall or under the floor where the ice has formed there is more ice built up on the coils. Keep applying heat to the area until all of the ice behind the wall is melted, which can take up to an hour or more. Aim the heat into the vents or air holes on the lower part of the wall or on the floor, depending on the model you have.

Once you have melted all the ice, turn the unit back on, be sure the freezer fan is running (that's the one inside the freezer compartment.) You should start to get cold air in the freezer in about an hour or two, and within 12 to 24 hours the temperatures should be normal. Once again this is only a temporary fix.

Other things that may cause a no cool problem are the freezer fan not running, a dirty condenser or the condenser fan not running, a bad compressor or bad starting components for the compressor, a bad cold control or thermostat.

First be sure your condenser (the coil under the refrigerator) is clean. This should be cleaned at least once a year, more often if you have pets.

Now check to see if the refrigerator is running. Most models built before 2002 the compressor, evaporator or freezer fan motor and the condenser fan motor should all be running at the same time. The condenser fan motor is located in the back next to the compressor. It has a small fan blade that is designed to keep the compressor cool when running. If one of these motors is running then all of them should be running.

If your refrigerator is plugged in and nothing is running you may have a bad cold control or thermostat or your defrost timer may be stuck in the defrost mode. Sometimes you can tap on the cold control or wiggle the knob to get the unit to start. If you do this and it starts running you will need to replace the control or have it replaced. If the defrost timer is stuck you will need to locate it to manually turn it out of defrost. Check your owner's manual for location.

If your refrigerator was built after 2002 or has electronic controls then you will need to call a qualified service technician. The electronic units have features that cause it to work different than the previous models.

5. Leaking water

If your refrigerator is leaking water on the floor there are some simple things to check.

First, do you have a water line connected to your refrigerator for an icemaker? If you do pull the refrigerator out from the wall and be sure the water line is not leaking. If the line is leaking or the connections at either end are leaking, you can buy a water line kit with new fittings at most home improvement or hardware stores. If the leak is not from the water line, look under the refrigerator with a flashlight to see if you can find anything dripping under the unit. There are plastic lines under the refrigerator that go to the icemaker or water dispenser if you have one.

Another common problem that causes leaks is a stopped up or frozen defrost drain. If this is the problem you will find ice built up on the floor in your freezer section if you have a side by side unit or water under your crispers in the bottom of your refrigerator if you have a top freezer. On the top freezer models you will have to take the back wall of the freezer and possibly the floor out to unstop the drain. If you are not sure how to remove the panels you should call for service.

If you have a side by side unit you can remove the bottom shelves or baskets in the freezer section and thaw out the ice with hot water or a hair dryer. After you get the ice out you will see a drain hole in the back just inside the section that the back wall is over. It is usually in the middle; if you can find this hole keep pouring hot water over it until it starts to drain. Keep bath towels in the bottom to catch the water until the drain is clear. If the ice is all melted and the drain is still stopped up you can stick your finger in the drain and plunge it with your finger to get it unstopped, or try using your shop vacuum to suck out the clog or the blower to push air through it.

Chapter 7
WASHERS

1. New versus old

2. Washer walks or vibrates

3. Clothes are tearing during wash

4. Washer won't go into rinse

5. Fabric softener won't dispense

6. Washer not spinning the clothes dry enough

7. Fills with water when it is not on

8. Leaks water on floor

9. Front load washers

1. Washers - new versus old

Your new washer is designed to get your clothes cleaner, spin your clothes dryer, use less energy, and give you more options. All for about the same money as you would have paid several years ago.

Here we will talk about top load machines. For front load machines see section 9.

Your new washer agitates and spins much faster than older machines. They also weigh a lot less. With that in mind you can expect to see and hear a lot more vibrating and movement in the newer machine.

Now let's talk about the floor under your machine. Remember your old washer weighed much more than the new one and the spin and agitate speeds were much slower. So just because your old machine worked fine in that spot does not mean your new washer will. If your new washer moves around a lot read section 2, "washer walks or vibrates," to determine if it is the machine or the floor causing the problem.

Now let's talk about one of the biggest problems that have been around for as long as I have been servicing washers.

Soap

Not that soap is the problem, but using too much soap is the problem.

Nobody thinks they use too much soap. I am going to give you a simple test you can do yourself that will let you know for sure whether you are wasting money on soap.

Keep in mind that I have been on several, and I do mean several, service calls that the problem was caused by, in a lot of cases the only problem, was too much soap being used. Those people had to pay for a service call so I could tell them that they were using too much soap. If you don't do anything else that I recommend in this book do this test. It may save you hundreds of dollars before you know it.

Before I give you the test information let me tell you what happens when you use too much soap. Your washer goes through the cycle, first it fills then it agitates, this is the wash cycle. Next it drains and spins. Then fills again and agitates again, this is the rinse cycle, then it drains and goes into the final spin. If you have one of the more expensive models you may have an extra rinse cycle that goes through the sequence again.

If you use too much soap you will still have soap in your clothes after the machine is done. You won't see it but it is there. You will also have soap left in the washer, down under the tub where you can't see it. The soap that is left in your clothes then gets dried into the fabric. This will cause your clothes to feel stiff or hard, sometimes even when you use fabric softener. This will also cause the fabric to break down sooner and your clothes will wear out faster and colors will not be as bright.

The soap that is left in your washer causes the seals to go out which causes leaks. It will build up in between the tubs and cause friction, which will cause it not to spin out at full speed. And the biggest problem is that you are wasting a lot of money buying more soap than you need.

Now, here is the test.

Take four to six clean bath towels out of your linen closet. Put them in your washer and do not add any soap or fabric softener. Set the water temperature for a hot water wash. Let the machine fill to the medium wash and let it agitate for about 5 minutes. Now look in the machine. See any soapsuds? If you don't see suds shut the machine off and wait till all the water has settled. Now look to see if you have soapy residue on the top of the water. If you see suds or soapy residue, you are using too much soap. What you are seeing is soap coming out of you clean towels, which means that soap was still in them after you finished washing them the last time.

I have had customers that have had to run their towels through as many as 8 times to get all the soap out. If you have soap left in your towels you probably have it in all your clothes. Before you can start using any soap again you first must get out all the soap remaining in the clothes. Keep in mind, more soap does not mean cleaner clothes. It means you will have soap left in your clothes after they have been washed. By using only what you need, your clothes will last longer and feel softer, your washer will last longer and you will not have to buy as much soap. It is possible you could save hundreds of dollars before you know it.

I know the owner's manual tells you to use a certain amount of soap. I have tested this at home. I found with soft water you can use about 1/8 to 1/4 of what they recommend and with hard water about 1/4 to 1/2 the recommended amount. You may have to experiment a little to get the right amount for your water condition.

Now many of you will say, "I use the same amount of soap I always did and I didn't have a problem before." Here are some of the reasons why the soap is a bigger factor than before. Soap is more concentrated than before, it is also scientifically designed to attack soil on clothes. If you are washing clothes without much soil, the soap doesn't break down. Your newer washer has a lot more plastic parts than the older washers and the plastic is more porous, so it will actually hold the extra soap in the plastic. Try the soap test. You might be surprised.

2. Washer walks or vibrates

A few things could cause this. If your washer is new be sure all the packing materials have been removed. Your new machine comes with an "owner's manual" and an "installation manual." In the installation manual there will be instructions on what packing has to be removed. It is very important to read this carefully and be sure to follow the steps. If the packing or shipping materials have not been removed, your washer will bang, jump, walk and act like it is possessed. Some companies will set up the unit for you if they deliver it to your house. Some companies just bring it in and leave it for you to set up. Be sure to find out if your delivery includes set up. Your manufactures warranty does not cover the cost of service to set up or install your unit.

Next, check to see if the unit is sitting level with all four legs sitting solid on the floor. Most washers have legs that twist in or out to get them level. There is a lock nut on that leg that needs to be tightened to the bottom of the washer to keep the leg tight. Some models only have adjusting legs on the front, so get these level and tight. To adjust the rear legs you will tip the washer forward on the two front legs, set it back easy onto the rear legs. These are called self-leveling legs. Your owner's manual or installation instructions will tell you if you have the self-leveling legs. Don't get confused by the self-leveling term. Only the rear legs have this feature. You must manually level and tighten the front legs.

Now you are sure the unit is installed and leveled correctly but it is still walking or vibrating too much. If you have a floor that has a slick or shinny surface you may need to add some non slip material to the bottom of the rubber feet on the washer. Remember your new washer spins at a much faster speed and weighs a lot less than an older machine. When it is loaded and spinning it will vibrate, which is normal. When the floor surface is slick the machine will shimmy out of its spot and become unleveled, causing it to walk or move across the floor.

You can use the same material that is used to keep throw rugs from slipping; it can be found at almost any store that sells throw rugs. Just cut a small piece and place it under each leg, which usually takes care of the problem.

If you are still having a problem, it may be that the floor has too much give in it for the newer lightweight washers. Padded flooring or carpet is not recommended. If your floor is slippery and has give in it, your washer will vibrate a lot more.

There is a simple test to see if your floor is soft. With the washer empty turn it to the spin cycle, set a glass of water on the dryer next to the washer or on the floor next to the washer. Turn the washer on. While the washer is spinning look to see if the water is moving in the glass on the dryer. The more the water jumps the softer your floor. If the floor is soft, that may be your only problem. There are some models that will operate on soft flooring without any problems, but if your washer is not one of those, there is not anything a service technician can do to make the machine stop moving.

Keep in mind that no matter how solid your floor is you will see some vibrating or movement of the cabinet on the washer, which is normal and will not cause anything to wear out or break.

You will also hear some strange noises on the newer washers. This is because you have less metal and faster moving parts. These noises are usually normal. You can look in the owner's manual or call the manufacture of your machine to find out if the noise is normal without having to pay a service call.

Be careful not to under load your machine. Too much water with smaller loads will cause an unleveled load. As the machine agitates the clothes move to one side. When the machine goes to spin, it becomes unbalanced.

3. Clothes are tearing during wash

There are a couple of things that can cause the washer to tear your clothes.

First there may be a ruff edge somewhere on the agitator. This can usually be filed down to smooth out the snag. Remember the newer washers agitate a lot faster so any ruff edges can cause problems.

Another possible cause is you are putting in too many clothes for the amount of water. You will notice most washers have a two piece agitator, designed to keep the clothes rotating to the bottom. If you get too many clothes in the machine they do not have any room to move. This will cause the agitator to work on the same clothes over and over and eventually tear them. Over loading is one of the most common things that happen. Another problem that occurs when you put in to many clothes is that they don't come as clean as they would if they could move and rotate.

You also need to be sure to set your controls to the right speed for the type of fabric. Light or thin materials should be washed on delicate or slow speed.

4. Washer won't go into rinse

The most common things that cause this to happen are a bad lid switch, a bad timer, or a bad water valve. All of these will require testing each component to determine which one is bad. There are a couple of things you can check before you call for service. Be sure you have cold water to the machine, most washers rinse in cold water only.

The easiest test for this is to set the washer for a cold wash cycle and set the timer at the normal wash cycle and turn it on, if your washer starts to fill with cold water then you know you have a good water supply and your water valve is good.

If you do not get water then you need shut the water off coming to the washer and remove the hose to the cold water at the back of the machine, it is marked on the machine which is cold and which is hot. Now put the end of the hose in a bucket and turn the water on. If you get water out then you know that your supply is good. You now will want to check where the hose was connected to the washer. There is a screen in the opening where the hose is attached to the washer with a flashlight look into the opening to be sure the screen is not stopped up. If it is, clean off the screen by gently scraping it with a small screw driver. Then reattach the hose and test again to see if the washer will fill with cold water. If you still do not get water you have a problem that will require service by a qualified service tech.

If your machine fills with cold water on the wash but still wont go into the rinse cycle you may have a bad lid switch, timer, or water valve.

5. Fabric softener won't dispense

If your machine has a fabric softener dispenser it is important to know that for the dispenser to work properly you must keep it clean.

Let's talk about how the dispenser works. If your dispenser is in the agitator it works by centrifugal force, when the machine goes into its spin before the rinse cycle, the spinning agitator forces the softener out of the cup. When the tub stops spinning the softener runs down the agitator through small holes into the bottom of the tub. If the dispenser is located somewhere else on the machine it fills with water to force the softener out, still through a small hole or hose.

Fabric softener is becoming more concentrated every year. This also means it is thicker and stickier than ever. The best advice I can give you is to dilute the softener before you put it in the dispenser. It does not take much softener to do the job if you are using the right amount of soap (read section 1 about soap.) All fabric softener dispensers will work better if you dilute the fabric softener.

The best way to dilute your softener is to pour part of the new bottle into a empty bottle and add water, and then each time you use the softener you should shake the bottle to get the softener mixed well before pouring it into the dispenser.

A lot of people think they are diluting the softener by pouring a small amount into the dispenser then adding the water in the dispenser. This does not work well because the softener is heavier than water and will stay at the bottom of the dispenser.

Most softeners should be diluted at least 2 to 1 to work properly in the dispenser. If you have soft water you can dilute 3 to 1 and still get good results. Remember if you have soft water you are only using the softener for the smell because if you are not using too much soap your clothes should already be soft.

6. Washer not spinning the clothes dry enough

This is a common complaint, and almost always due to using too much soap.

If there is too much soap left in the clothes after the final rinse the soapsuds will cause a restriction between the spin basket and the outer tub and cause the tub to spin slower and not extract all the water from the clothes. To see if you are using too much soap go back to section 1 of this chapter and follow the test instructions.

If you find you are not using too much soap you may have a worn belt or clutch. Either of these will require service from a qualified service tech.

7. Fills with water when it is not on

This condition is caused by a defective water valve. You can turn off the water supply to the washer to stop the water from coming in. The water valve will have to be replaced to correct the problem.

8. Leaks water on the floor

There are a few things to look for when this occurs. First check the two fill hoses connected to the back of the washer. Be sure to check both ends where they are connected. If there is any moisture around the ends you probably need to replace the rubber washers in the end of the hoses. These are the same type of washers found in the end of your garden hose. If there is no moisture present at the ends of the hoses, check to make sure the drain hose has not worked its way partially out of the drain. If the drain hose is not positioned in the drain properly water will splash out over the drain and onto the floor during the drain cycle. Also, watch the water drain out into the drain for the full drain cycle of the washer to be sure the water is not over flowing from your house drain. I have been on numerous service calls for leaky washers just to find out the drain line in the house was backing up causing the drain to overflow. To be sure it is the washer leaking pull the unit out from the wall about a foot.

Have a flashlight handy and watch the drain and the floor behind the washer during the drain/spin cycle to be sure the water leaking is coming from the machine and not the drain or wall behind the machine. This requires a little more work on your behalf but it is a lot cheaper than paying a service call to a tech just to find out you have to call a plumber.

If you find that the water is actually coming from the washer it could be one of several parts. The most common parts to cause a leak are the pump, water valve, or a bad hose. You could also have bad seals or a hole in your outer tub. Most of these will require calling for service.

9. Front load washers

Front load washers have been around for many years but only recently have they become popular as a household appliance. There are a lot of benefits to front load washers. They save a tremendous amount of water and are gentler on your clothes and they use less soap.

Now with all that in mind also take into consideration that they cost a lot more up front and when they need service they usually cost more to repair.

Even with the higher cost there is no doubt that they are a lot gentler on your clothing. They do not use an agitator so there is less wear on the clothing. Front loaders also extract a lot more water in the final spin to give you shorter drying cycles.

The most common service call on front loaders has to do with the user, not the machine. Not that the machines never have a problem, but people don't want to read the owners manual or watch the video that comes with the machine, even though they have just spent a lot of extra money for a machine that is built different from anything they have ever used.

That's right! The new front loaders are built different from anything else you have ever used. People tell me all the time that they used the front loaders at the laundry-mat. Those commercial front loaders are nothing like the ones built for your home. Even the older front loaders that were built for your home are nothing like the ones built today.

The first thing to remember is that you are using about 1/3 the water that you would in a top loader so you have to use about 1/3 the amount of soap. (be sure to read section 1 of this chapter about using too much soap) The same goes for bleach and fabric softener, you have to use less or you <u>will</u> have problems.

Another important thing to remember is that because you are not submersing your clothes in a tub full of water you will have to pretreat most stains, this is covered in your owners manual.

Front loaders have computers to help with all the functions and energy savings. These same computers will keep the machine from completing certain cycles if the computer detects that you have too much soap in the system, or the load is not balanced. Keep in mind that you cannot do a real small load or the clothes will not balance and the computer will not let the machine spin out properly. There has to be enough clothing in the machine to balance the tub when it goes into the spin cycle. This means there has to be enough clothing that, when wet, it will cover the tub all the way around when spinning. You cannot wash just a couple of pieces. The machine has to detect a balanced load before it will go into a full spin.

It is hard to overload a front load washer but it is very easy to under load one

The flooring under your machine must also be good and solid. Front load machines will not work properly on soft flooring. This includes carpet and laminate or floating floors. If the machine is not level or if the floor under the machine is not solid the machine will vibrate excessively and may bounce or walk when trying to spin.

The best advice I can give you is if you are going to spend the money on a front load washer, read the owners manual or if your machine comes with a video watch it <u>before</u> you use the machine. Keep in mind that your warranty <u>does not</u> cover a service tech coming to your home to instruct you on how to use your machine.

I am a big fan of front load washers because of the savings of energy, both water and electricity. Just keep in mind that these machines like any other sophisticated piece of machinery have a lot more electronics and will be costlier to repair.

Chapter 8
FURNACES

The most neglected and hardest worked appliance in your home is usually your furnace. Most people believe their furnace should last a lifetime. The older your furnace is the more energy it uses.

Today's newer furnaces, like all other appliances, have more electronics and are much more energy efficient, it is one of the appliances in your home that most people don't think about until it won't work. If your furnace is over twenty years old it may be time to start looking at replacing it. Older furnaces use a lot more energy to heat your home and the older they are the more this is true.

Your furnace should be serviced at least once every two years. If your furnace is more than ten years old you should have it checked every year to be sure it is operating properly. This needs to be done by a qualified service tech. There are a few things you can do to help prolong the life of your furnace. The most important thing is to keep the filter clean or replaced. Most heating systems have a filter that can be replaced fairly easy. Most service techs will be happy to show you how to change your own filter. If it is too difficult for you to change, check into having a different filter rack installed. It might be worth the cost to be able to change your own filter. You also need to keep the area around the furnace clean and the return air vents clean and open.

If you have a gas furnace be sure you own a carbon dioxide tester and, just like your smoke detector, check it often to be sure it is in working order. You can find these just about any place that smoke detectors are sold. If your furnace is leaking carbon dioxide into your home these detectors will let you know. If your detector goes off, be sure to call a qualified service tech immediately to have your furnace checked.

Chapter 9
AIR CONDITIONERS

If you want your air conditioner to operate properly and last for many years it must be cleaned every year. This is true with window air conditioners as well as central air conditioner systems. You can do this yourself or call a professional if you are not comfortable doing it. Either way it is important to do it at least once a year, more often if you are lucky enough to live where you use your air conditioner year round.

The coils on the air conditioner are what need to be kept clean. The coils are the aluminum fins on the front and back of window air conditioners and usually around the sides on central air conditioners. The easiest way to do this is with a water hose. First be sure the power is disconnected or the unit is unplugged. If it is a window unit it should be removed from the window. With a nozzle on the end of the hose, spray the water pressure into and through the coils. What you are trying to do is to flush the dirt through the coils. To do this, place the nozzle about 12 inches away from the coil and flush the water through with up and down strokes following the pattern of the coils. If the coils start bending you are too close with the nozzle. Just back it away until the water pressure doesn't bend the coils.

If you clean your coils regularly it will help with the over all operation of your air conditioner. You also need to clean or replace the filter, on window units or the furnace filter for central units.

Air conditioners should not have to be recharged often. When you have your unit serviced, if you are being charged to have refrigerant added to your system then you need to find out why. Air conditioning systems, both window and central, do not use up refrigerant or Freon. If your system is low and needs to be recharged there has to be a leak in the system. If you do not have the leak found and fixed, you will not only continue to throw money away on the recharge, you are allowing contamination or moisture to enter the system through the leak which can ruin the entire system. If your air conditioner does not have a leak, you should not have to add more to the system. Be wary of service companies that are always charging to add Freon.

Chapter 10
TRASH COMPACTORS

Trash compactors do not require much maintenance other than keeping the slides for the bin cleaned. You should remove the bin at least once a month and clean the area behind the bin and around the slides to keep the unit working properly. Trash can work its way over the bin during normal operation and cause the bin to jam or stick. Read your owners manual to find out how the bin comes out then be sure to follow the directions for cleaning. Most service calls on trash compactors are due to the build up of trash behind the bin or around the slides for the bin.

There are other things that can cause the machine to jam or stick, such as, putting plastic or glass bottles or jugs in the compactor. These items can wedge themselves between the compactor plate and the side of the bin. This can cause serious damage to the gears and motor and be a very expensive repair. Regardless of what the owner's manual says you can put in the compactor, I advise my customers to use their compactors for paper products and garbage. Keep the cans, glass, and plastics out of the compactor.

Chapter 11
ICE MACHINES

If you use a lot of ice there is nothing like an ice machine. I am not talking about an ice maker in your freezer; I am talking about a free standing ice machine.

There are two types of ice machines that are made for household use. One requires electric, a water supply, and a drain. The other type requires electric and a water supply. Let's talk about the one with a drain first.

These machines often called "clear ice" or "fresh ice" machines. They are a high maintenance item. They must be cleaned on a regular basis. How often they will need to be cleaned depends on the quality of water being supplied to the machine. One of the things people like the most about this type of machine is that it produces fresh ice as needed to keep the bin full, and the ice does not stick together. These machines work the same as the commercial type ice machines, only on a smaller scale. The storage bin is not refrigerated, they are just insulated. As the old ice on the bottom melts, the new "fresh ice" is dropped on top. This is why the machine has to have a drain. It is also why, even if you do not use any ice from this machine, it will come on and run to refill the bin from the "old ice" melting off. The

63

newer machines with electronic controls have a cleaning cycle that makes it easy for the owner to do the cleaning themselves. With service companies charging $100 and more each time they clean your machine, this can save hundreds of dollars in service over the years. The important thing to remember is that it will have to be cleaned by someone at least once a year if you have really good water. If you have hard water, it will have to be cleaned several times a year. A water softener will help; having a filter system designed for an ice machine with the softener will help even more. Remember even with the best water, you will have to clean the machine at least 1 time every 12 months. Your owner's manual will give you directions for cleaning your machine. Some machines have the instructions printed on the door. If you do not have instructions for your machine, you should call the manufacturer of your machine and have them send you a manual. Most manufacturers will do this for a very small fee, some for free.

Along with keeping the water flow system cleaned, your ice machine has a condenser coil much like your refrigerator has that needs to be cleaned at least once a year. This is located at the bottom of the machine usually in the front. Keeping the condenser clean will keep the compressor running at the proper temperatures and prolong the life of your machine.

The other type of ice machine that is made for the home requires less maintenance and works much like the one in your freezer. This machine has an ice maker head much like the head a normal refrigerator/freezer. The storage bin for the ice is kept at freezing temperatures so the ice does not melt off. If you do not use much ice, the ice in the bin will sometimes stick together or ice cubes will partiality evaporate. The up-side to this type of machine is it does not run as much if you are not using much ice and it does not require cleaning the water flow system. Good water is just as important in this type of machine. Hard water can damage the head of the ice maker, and the cost to repair or replace the head is almost as much as replacing the machine. You still have to clean the condenser at least once a year.

Chapter 12
FINDING A QUALIFIED
AND HONEST
SERVICE COMPANY

There are a lot of honest people in the service industry. Unfortunately there are also some not so honest. It is impossible to know who you can trust. The best advice I can give you is to do a little research before you set up a service call. Check with friends, co-workers or relatives to find out if they have had a good experience with a certain company. If you end up going to the yellow pages like most people, be sure to ask some questions about the company before you set up a service call. What is the total charge just to come to your house and diagnose the problem? What is the address of the company? How long have they been in business? Who is the person coming to your house to do the service? What is the warranty or guarantee on the service they are going to do? Check out several companies in your area before you make your decision.

Most people look for a service company in the local phone books. There are a few tips to remember when you are looking through the ads. First thing to keep in mind is that there are **no free service calls**. You will see ads that say this, but if you read carefully or ask when you call the company you will find that there are conditions to that <u>free</u> word. Another thing that is somewhat misleading to consumers is the local phone numbers. People see a local phone number listed and they believe they are dealing with a local company.

First let's talk about the "free service call." That is a gimmick used by companies to get their foot in the door. They will tell you the service call is free if they do the repair. If the repair is too expensive and you don't want to fix it, then they charge you a service call and, in some cases, it is a lot more than the average charged by most honest service companies. If you do decide to have the repair, the price you pay will have the (service call) built in. Be sure to ask when setting up the service call what the charge will be if you do not do the repair. Another thing to watch for is an unusually high estimate of the repair. There are techs that will give an outrageous estimate if they do not know how to fix the appliance or they don't want to fix it. Some techs only want to do the fast easy repairs. It is sometimes wise to get a second opinion. A good tip to remember is that you should stay with in view of the service tech during the repair. Not that you need to be looking over his shoulder, but you should be close enough to have a conversation if needed. Sometimes the tech may have questions for you as he is working on the unit that may help with identifying the problem. It is good practice to stay fairly close by. Don't be afraid to ask questions to the tech about the repair. If the tech is being honest with you about everything they should have no trouble answering your questions. If at any time you think the tech is not being honest or trying to scam you, you should tell them you have decided not to do the repair right now or that you are going to get a second opinion before spending that much on the repair. You may have to pay an extra service call, but in some cases that may still be cheaper that going ahead with the repair from the first company. As an example, I got a call from a woman that explained to me that she had her refrigerator repaired a few weeks earlier. The company she had called had replaced a part and charged her $328.00. It seemed to work ok for about 2 weeks, then it quit cooling again. She called them several times and kept getting the runaround. After a week she gave up and decided to try someone else. Once I found the problem the repair was less than $150.00 and the part installed by the other company was not the part needed. As we were talking she told me she was a little leery about the first estimate, she felt like the tech was hustling her. Remember, you are the customer. If you are not comfortable with your technician, send him on his way and get someone else. If a part is replaced, be sure to keep the old part for thirty days.

Now let's talk about the phone numbers. Just because a company has a local phone number does not mean that they are in or even close to your area. Companies can get phone numbers for any area they want and as many different numbers as they can afford. Just because you see phone numbers listed in their advertisements for several different locations or areas doesn't mean they have multiple physical locations to go with those phone numbers.

Another thing misleading to consumers is the size of the ad. Most consumers think the larger the ad the bigger the company and they believe the bigger the company the better the chance of getting honest and quality service. The fact is that a lot of the biggest ads are from the smaller companies with the owner also being the technician. This can be a good thing if they are honest. You can check with your local Better Business Bureau or attorney generals office to find out if the company has a list of complaints. But keep in mind that some companies out there change their names every couple of years, so there may be complaints on the former name but nothing on the recent one. Researching all of that is very time consuming and if your appliance is broken you need to get it fixed now. So ask the questions listed in the beginning of this section up front. Stay close by when the service tech gets there. Ask to be given an estimate of exactly what repair is needed and how much it will cost before the repair is done. Let them know you want to keep the all parts that are replaced. Any qualified service tech should be able to do all of this, which should help minimize your chance of being ripped off.

The size of the company is not as important as the quality of the technician. There are some pretty large companies out there that have some pretty shady techs. Any time you are not satisfied with the service you need to call and file a complaint. If the company has multiple techs ask for the supervisor. If the company is a one or two man operation and you do not get satisfaction from the owner file a complaint with the local Better Business Bureau or with the local attorney general. If you don't take the time to call in your complaint, then no one will know that this company or tech is being dishonest, leaving the door open for the next victim. Unfortunately it is not considered a crime in most areas to over charge a customer or give bad service. The only way to help stop this is to take time to make the call.

Thank you for purchasing this book. By following the tips in each chapter you will save money and make your appliances last longer. Good luck and may God bless.

About the Author

Vernon Schmidt has serviced major household appliances and heating/air conditioning since 1974, first servicing appliances and equipment for a national fast food chain. He started a repair business part-time which turned full-time in 1980, has serviced about every brand appliance manufactured and is factory authorized to service products under warranty. He trains new appliance technicians and attends new product training courses several times a year.

"It would be nice to know things a good service technician knows, before buying an appliance or calling for service," his customers suggested. He wrote his book with as much information as possible, that the homeowner could understand, use to save money when repairing appliances, and obtain helpful tips on buying appliances

Printed in the United States
81661LV00001B/171

9 781420 834543